W9-BUM-654

0 00 30 0218622 3

98

DATE DUE

j616.043 Landau, Elaine.
LAN
            Joined at birth

HAYNER PUBLIC LIBRARY DISTRICT
ALTON, ILLINOIS

OVERDUES .10 PER DAY. MAXIMUM FINE
COST OF BOOKS. LOST OR DAMAGED BOOKS
ADDITIONAL $5.00 SERVICE CHARGE.

JOINED AT BIRTH

JOINED AT BIRTH

THE LIVES OF
CONJOINED TWINS

BY ELAINE LANDAU

A First Book

FRANKLIN WATTS   A Division of Grolier Publishing
New York / London / Hong Kong / Sydney / Danbury, Connecticut

HAYNER PUBLIC LIBRARY DISTRICT
ALTON, ILLINOIS

FOR LUIS ADRIAN

Subject Consultant
JOE J. HOO, M.D.
Professor of Pediatrics, Director of Genetics
SUNY Health Science Center, Syracuse, NY

Cover illustration ©: Victoria Vebell
Photographs ©: Columbia Presbyterian Medical Center: 28 (Rene Perez); Impact Visuals: 44, 46, 47, 49, 51 (Steve Wewerka); Medical Photography: 35 (Oscar Suerdo); North Carolina Collection, University of N.C. Library at Chapel Hill: 8, 17; North Carolina Department of Cultural Resources, Division of Archives & History: 14, 19; Photo Researchers: 24 (Alan Carruthers), 29 (Hank Morgan/SS); Reuters/Corbis-Bettmann: 32, 37; Robert Clink: 38; The Southern Historical Collection, University of North Carolina at Chapel Hill: 16; Texas Children's Hospital: 26 (Paul Vincent Kuntz), 22 (James de Leon); Visuals Unlimited: 12 (Science/VU), 33 (SIU).

Library of Congress Cataloging-in-Publication Data

Landau, Elaine.
Joined at birth : the lives of conjoined twins / by Elaine Landau.
p. cm. — (A first book)
Includes bibliographical references and index.
Summary: Explores the issue of conjoined twins, including a discussion of the difficult decision regarding physical separation that parents must face.
ISBN 0-531-20331-X
1. Siamese twins—Juvenile literature. [1. Siamese twins.]
I. Title. II. Series.
QM691.L36 1997
616.043—dc20
                                                                    96-38707
                                                                        CIP
                                                                         AC

© 1997 by Elaine Landau
All rights reserved. Published simultaneously in Canada
Printed in the United States of America
1 2 3 4 5 6 7 8 9 10 R 06 05 04 03 02 01 00 99 98 97

j616.043
LAN

ACY-3429

CONTENTS

JOINED AT BIRTH

Eng and Chang were connected for life by a short, wide band of flesh.

CHAPTER 1

ENG
&
CHANG

*T*his story begins on a small bamboo houseboat floating on a quiet river in the far eastern country of Siam (now Thailand). There, on May 11, 1811, a woman gave birth to twin sons. Although the delivery went smoothly, the mood in the room soon turned from joy to shock and disbelief.

The **midwife** and others there had never seen twins like these before. While the boys were perfectly formed, their bodies were connected at the breast bone by a short, wide band of flesh.

The unusual birth caused quite a stir in the country. A number of area doctors flocked to see the babies named Eng, on the left, and Chang, on the right. Some said the children should be separated. But the means suggested seemed so harsh and painful that the boys' parents decided to leave the twins as they were.

During their infancy and childhood, Eng and Chang continued to attract attention. Visitors from distant parts of Siam who came to see them spoke about the experience for years. The king of Siam even invited the boys to court so that he could view them himself.

Despite the fleshy band connecting them, the brothers learned to walk, run, swim, and handle a fishing boat. In time, they grew muscular and strong working alongside their fisher father. Sometimes the boys squabbled. But arguing was hard on them, because the two couldn't spend any time apart to calm down. Therefore, as very young children, they learned to compromise.

Their father died in 1819 during a cholera **epidemic** when Eng and Chang were just eight years old. The twins couldn't afford to be a village **curiosity** any longer.

They had to grow up quickly to help their family survive. Because the boys already knew how to fish, they went to work for a local fisher. Yet Eng and Chang knew they could do better on their own. So they saved part of their earnings to buy a small boat and went into business for themselves.

The family's finances improved somewhat, but the boys' lifestyle did not drastically change until the twins came to the attention of an American trader named Abel Coffin. Coffin, whose business dealings frequently brought him to Siam, saw the now-seventeen-year-old twins as a lucrative show-business property. After he secured the king of Siam's permission to exhibit the boys in the United States, he proposed the idea to the twins and their mother.

Eng and Chang were thrilled at the prospect of visiting America, but their mother had her doubts. She was concerned about how her sons would endure the long sea voyage, how they would like America, and how she and her younger children would survive without the twins' income. But Coffin assured her that Eng and Chang would be well cared for. She was also given five hundred dollars, a fairly large sum at the time, for her family to live on during the boys' absence.

Eng and Chang, who came to be known as the Siamese twins, attracted thousands of spectators. Charging fifty cents to view the boys, Coffin packed

This poster for the twins' first U.S. tour could be purchased by audience members.

huge crowds into a circus tent he set up in Boston. When skeptics questioned whether the **ligament** connecting the twins was real, Coffin called in a well-respected surgeon to examine the boys. Once the doctor confirmed that they were genuinely attached, Eng and Chang's popularity soared.

After completing a successful U.S. tour, Coffin booked the twins abroad. He felt that a British tour might put them in even greater demand when they returned to America. But on the voyage to England, the twins became dismayed with Coffin. While he and his family stayed in luxurious first-class cabins and feasted on sumptuous meals and snacks, the twins' accommodations were significantly inferior. They traveled steerage class and were only given salt beef and potatoes, which they ate with the crew.

When Eng and Chang questioned Coffin about their poor treatment, he said it was the ship captain's fault. But this wasn't true. The boys later learned that Coffin had paid nearly nothing for their passage. They also discovered that while their mother had only received five hundred dollars, Coffin told newspapers that he had given her three thousand.

To add to the injustice, Coffin only paid the twins a fraction of what they earned. Coffin also overworked the boys and severely disciplined them for even the

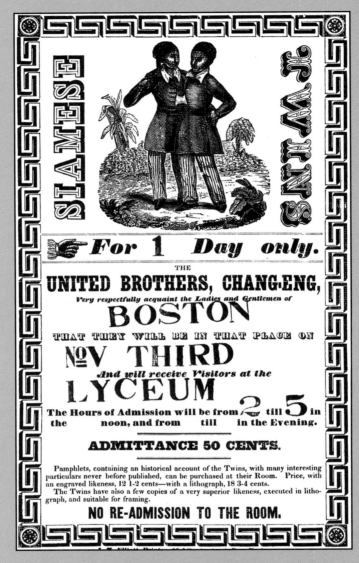

As seen on this handbill, Bostonians paid fifty-cents admission to see the twins.

slightest error. But despite their resentment, Eng and Chang were unable to break away from Coffin until they turned twenty-one. At that point, they were no longer minors and thus legally free of Coffin's supervision.

As adults, Eng and Chang greatly enhanced their lives by managing their own tours. Before long, they had made enough money to buy a farm in North Carolina. Both looked forward to earning a living without having to display themselves. While most people thought the twins would never marry, two sisters from a respectable Southern family became their brides. Between them, Eng and Chang fathered twenty-one children.

Both families started out living in the same house. As the families grew, however, the living quarters became extremely cramped. Eng and Chang built a larger house, but tensions between the couples still ran high. The twins continued to get along fairly well with one another, but the same wasn't always true for their wives. Although the women were sisters, at times they felt that they simply saw too much of each other. Each wanted to run her household and raise her children as she saw fit, but this was often impossible in their situation.

Attempting to improve matters, Eng and Chang moved their families into separate homes. The twins

The twins' North Carolina farm

spent three days at Chang's house with his wife and children, and then moved to Eng's home for the next three days. The men rigidly followed this schedule regardless of illness, inclement weather, or holidays.

But after a time, Eng and Chang found that they weren't able to stay very long at either house. With twenty-one children to educate, the twin brothers realized that they needed more money than their farm yielded. Therefore, to meet their families' financial needs, the twins began touring the United States again. They returned home as often as possible, but they were still away a great deal.

Eng and Chang's wives were from a respectable Southern family.

Eng and Chang pose with two of their children. Notice how much the boys look like their fathers.

With so little time to spend with each family, Eng and Chang began to consider seriously the question that others had asked them all their lives. Could they be surgically separated? Medicine had advanced through the years, but doctors were still quick to point out that severing the twins would be extremely risky. While on the outside it looked as though they were merely connected by a fleshy band, they actually shared a liver. Doctors were doubtful that this vital organ could be successfully split between Eng and Chang. The brothers could not find a physician who would separate them unless one of them died. It was reasoned that at that point, the other would surely die if their bodies weren't split apart.

Eng and Chang died on July 17, 1874, at the age of sixty-three. As it happened, Chang's health failed before his brother's. After a restless night, Chang died in his sleep. The doctor who came to separate the twins arrived too late. Eng only lived for about an hour after Chang's death. Nothing was left to do but examine their corpses and officially pronounce the brothers dead.

Eng and Chang in their later years

To some extent, Eng and Chang were victims of the limited medical and scientific knowledge of their time. If they had been born a century later, they might have been separated successfully as other conjoined twins sharing a liver have been.

CHAPTER 2

CONJOINED TWINS

*A*ll children born physically joined were once referred to as Siamese twins. Today, the term Siamese twins is no longer used because it is considered degrading. Instead, twins born attached to one another are referred to by the medical term—conjoined twins.

Conjoined twins are rare. Only about one out of every half million births each year results in conjoined twins. The condition occurs between the thirteenth and fifteenth day after **conception** in a women's womb carrying identical twins. At this time, the early embryo fails to divide cleanly and entirely as it should. Because these twins develop from a single egg, the children are the same sex and have the same blood type. But unlike other identical twins, they don't separate completely.

Five-month-old conjoined twins

Conjoined twins may be attached in more than a dozen ways. Twins joined at the chest and abdomen are the most common. **Dicephalic twins**, those who have two heads but share one two-legged body, are the most unusual. For some unknown reason, the majority of conjoined twins are female.

Most conjoined twins are surgically separated during infancy if the procedure is medically possible in their case. The odds of both twins surviving the surgery depends on the manner in which they are connected and the organs shared. The first such successful surgery was performed in Europe in 1689 when twins joined at the naval by a single band of flesh were separated. But in most instances, the operation is extremely risky. It is estimated that in approximately three hundred years of medical history, only about one hundred twins have been parted successfully. Unfortunately, often only one twin survives the operation. In the worst cases, both babies die.

There are still some encouraging accounts of operations that have succeeded. Two-year-old conjoined twins Rosa and Carmen Traveras of the Dominican Republic had their surgery performed at Babies Hospital of the Columbia Presbyterian Medical Center in New York City. The Traveras twins were joined at the hip—sharing a pelvis and several internal organs. If

they were left connected, neither would ever be able to sit, stand, or walk.

A team of fifty medical professionals, including an assortment of physicians, nurses, and therapists, were assembled for the operation. The twins' separation also involved the use of high-tech equipment, labs, and a stay in the intensive care unit at a cost of more than 1,000 dollars a day. A good deal of testing was done prior to the actual surgery. It was crucial that the surgeons knew exactly which organs were joined as well as their precise placement.

On the day of the surgery, the girls were wheeled into the operating room at 7:30 A.M. By 2:30 P.M., they were separate individuals. But the doctors were far from finished. They still had to reconstruct the girls' pelvises and deal with any obstacles that arose.

Luckily, there were no major problems. The twins recovered speedily following the surgery. Hospital nurses placed them in their cribs so that they could see and hear one another. As one of the surgeons described the children's reactions, "They love being separated. They interact and play with joy."[1] Everyone reported

Conjoined twins are always of the same gender and have the same blood type.

Like Rosa and Carmen Traveras, two-year-old twins Iesha (left) and Tiesha (right) were separated successfully. Here, they play together before Iesha is taken to surgery for a minor operation.

that the girls took obvious pleasure in being able to stretch and move in ways they hadn't been able to before.

The surgical results weren't as ideal for Millie and Lucy Castillo, another set of female conjoined twins from the Dominican Republic. The twins were joined from the collar bone to the naval and needed more complex surgery than the Traveras twins. The doctors couldn't predict with certainty that both children would survive the operation. Nevertheless, it was generally agreed among the doctors that the girls needed to be separated. If either died of heart trouble or a serious upper respiratory infection as they were, the other would perish as well.

As with the Traveras girls, the doctors carefully tested and examined the Castillo twins. They were especially anxious to learn whether the girls' hearts were joined. It was impossible to know if they had one or two hearts, or how difficult it might be to separate a connected heart, until the twins were on the operating table.

Once the surgery began, the doctors were pleased to find that Millie and Lucy's hearts were completely separate. One of the hearts had merely been lying on top of the other, making it look as though they were joined.

The surgeons still had to complete the delicate process of separating the girls' livers. Although in similar attempts some children had died of massive blood loss, Millie and Lucy survived this step. Now all that was left to do was to close the large hole left in their chest walls where they had been attached.

Everything appeared to be going well until Millie unexpectedly stopped breathing on the operating table.

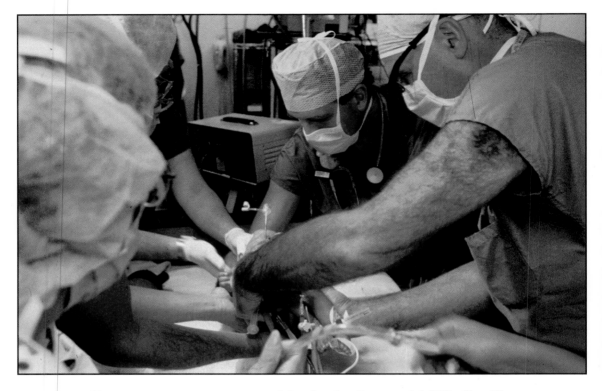

Doctors operate to separate conjoined twins Lucy and Millie Castillo.

The medical team revived and stabilized her. Before long, Lucy and Millie were both resting comfortably in the intensive care unit. For the first time in their lives, they fell asleep in separate cribs.

It looked as though the girls would be coming home soon. But they were not out of danger. Lucy was recovering as expected, but Millie had become quite ill. Her lungs weren't functioning as well as they should have been. The doctors didn't know why this was happening, but it was clear that Millie was going to have to fight for her life.

Despite the risk involved, the surgeons decided to reopen Millie's chest to see if an infection had set in. But the surgery failed to provide even a clue as to why Millie was so ill. Days passed and she still didn't respond to treatment.

Some surgeries to separate conjoined twins have been extremely successful. The twins shown here with their parents were formerly joined at their heads.

In a final effort to save Millie, she was put on an ECMO (Extra Corporal Membranous Oxygenation)— a machine that acts as an artificial lung. This would give her lungs a chance to rest and heal. But thirty-four days after the separation surgery, Millie's lungs still hadn't improved. She experienced bleeding, and her small body swelled. Convinced that being on an ECMO had become more harmful than helpful, the doctors took Millie off the machine. Now they could only hope that the child's own lungs would sustain her. But Millie simply wasn't strong enough. She died shortly thereafter. Her doctors aren't certain why Millie's lungs never recovered following her separation from Lucy.

Despite the outcome, Dr. Peter Altman, one of the twins' surgeons, does not regret the decision to operate. He noted, "I have no hesitation and I don't lament at all the decision to undertake separation. Many others involved in the decision, including the family, are absolutely convinced that that was the right thing to do. It's not easy . . . but it gets easier, I guess, when we go up and see Lucy."[2]

CHAPTER 3

QUESTIONS & CONCERNS

*T*he general trend today is to separate conjoined twins whenever possible. But this choice has sometimes been questioned. One highly publicized case that raised some important moral and ethical concerns involved conjoined twins Angela and Amy Lakeberg.

Ken and Reitha Lakeberg talk with reporters at a press conference.

Ken and Reitha Lakeberg learned that they were having conjoined twins through an ultrasound test Reitha took during her thirteenth week of pregnancy. The doctors felt it was extremely unlikely that both children would live and added that there was probably

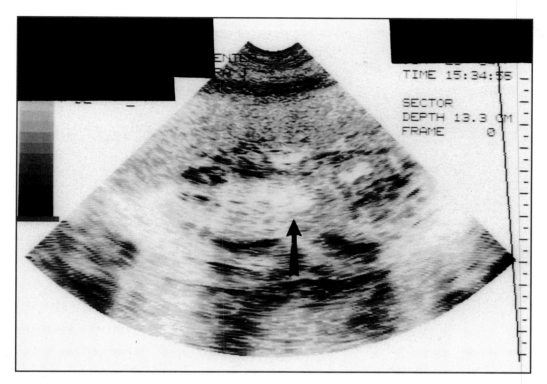

Reitha Lakeberg learned she was having conjoined twins through an ultrasound test, such as this one. The arrow is pointing to where the children are connected.

only about a 20 percent chance of even one twin surviving. They brought up the option of ending the pregnancy, and at first the Lakebergs agreed. The Wheatfield, Indiana, couple's financial situation was not ideal at the time, and they already had a five-year-old daughter to care for. Yet the Lakebergs later indicated that they never really felt comfortable with the decision.

When Reitha went to the clinic for the procedure, her appointment was postponed because the staff wasn't prepared to handle her complex pregnancy. But it didn't matter, because the Lakebergs changed their minds and decided to have the twins. As Mrs. Lakeberg described her feelings, "In my heart, I couldn't get rid of my babies."[1]

On June 29, 1993, she gave birth to twin girls, Angela and Amy, weighing a total of just more than 9 pounds (4.1 kg). Shortly after they were born, the doctors realized that the girls had even more serious medical problems than they had anticipated. Like many conjoined twins, Angela and Amy shared a liver. But the greatest obstacle to their survival was that they had only one heart between them. Unfortunately, the heart they shared was not even a healthy one. A normal heart has four chambers, but the twins had a six-chambered heart, and one of its chambers had a hole in it.

Doctors saw little hope for the Lakeberg babies and felt that they would never survive surgical separation. Experts stressed that one twin would surely die on the operating table, while it was unlikely that the other would live very long thereafter. Under the circum-

Dr. Jonathan Muraskas at a press conference at Loyola University Medical Center in suburban Chicago

stances, the medical team suggested that they not attempt to prolong the girls' lives. "We sort of pleaded with them [the twins' parents] to take the babies off the ventilator," recalled Dr. Jonathan Muraskas of Loyola University Medical Center in suburban Chicago. "Let's feed them and keep them warm," he suggested. "Let's put them in God's hands, so to speak."[2] Dr. Muraskas stressed that separating conjoined twins sharing a heart had only been done six previous times. Out of those surgeries, the longest a surviving twin had lived was three months.

The Lakebergs were willing to try anything to give the twins a chance, however. "I can't live my life wondering if one of them, with that chance, would have lived," the girls' mother had said.[3] As a result, the babies were flown in a specially equipped jet to Children's Hospital in Philadelphia, Pennsylvania. A team of pediatric surgeons there had previously separated a number of conjoined twins.

The situation still wasn't promising. Some doctors estimated that there was only about a 1 percent chance of a single twin surviving very long after surgery. No one knew of a separated twin with a defective heart who had lived long enough to attend elementary school. There was also the inescapable question of cost. The estimated price of the girls' surgery and care was more than a million dollars.

Nevertheless, the doctors at Children's Hospital agreed to respect the parents' wishes and operate. Their decision sparked a national debate about health care and medical options in America. Because the Lakebergs did not have health insurance, the money

Ken Lakeberg speaks to the press regarding his daughters' surgery.

had to come from other sources. This meant that tax-payer dollars combined with some limited funds set aside for needy patients at the hospital would be used to pay the bill.

With the skyrocketing costs of health care in America, some people felt it wasteful to spend such a large sum of money when the odds for success were so poor. They argued that the money would have been better spent elsewhere. "There are kids with no tetanus shots, moms who have never been to a doctor or who have just given birth and don't know how to feed their babies, and no resources are pointing in those

Arthur Caplan addresses an audience at a conference at the University of Pennsylvania Medical Center.

directions," stressed Arthur Caplan, director of the University of Minnesota's Center for Biomedical Ethics.[4]

It was also argued that physicians have an obligation not to perform surgery when there's almost no chance for a desirable outcome. This led some people to ask if something should be done just because it could be done. Rather than be guided by the parents' wishes, a number of **ethicists** believe the medical community must do what is prudent and reasonable. They feel that this is especially important in crisis situations when a distraught parent's judgment might be clouded by anxiety or guilt.

As one bioethicist suggested, "You've got to present options in a way that lets doctors bear the responsibility and the burden."[5] This means that high-risk surgery, such as that of the Lakeberg twins, should not be described to families as sound medical practice but rather as a learning experience for the medical community. This opinion was underscored by Dr. John LaPuma, an ethicist at Chicago's Lutheran General Hospital, who said, "Parents like the Lakebergs should be told that the surgery that their babies would undergo is a research experiment, not a treatment. . . . It shouldn't be portrayed as being for the babies' good."[6]

The Lakeberg twins' surgery brought up still other

troubling issues. It was impossible to split the girls' poorly functioning heart between them. Therefore, one twin would have to die to improve the other's odds for survival. But is it morally acceptable to take the life of one child to try to save another? There is also the question of the extent of health care to which every person should be entitled. Should there be limits? And if limits aren't imposed, how can costs be met?

Despite the arguments against it, the Lakebergs decided to proceed with the surgery. "People win the lottery every week. Why can't we?" the twins' father had responded when reminded of the odds.[7]

The surgery to separate the Lakeberg twins involved eighteen doctors and took about five and a half hours. The girls' liver was divided before the surgeons began reconstructing the twins' damaged heart. As expected, one of the twins, Amy, died during the operation. But the surviving twin, Angela, came through the procedure better than expected. As her father, Ken Lakeberg, described his daughter shortly after surgery, "She looks good. She's got color. She opened her eyes just briefly, and then went back to sleep of course. But we got to hold her hand and stroke her hair and she looks good."[8]

Angela lived a full ten months following separation from her twin. To those who cared for Angela during her lengthy hospital stay, the child's death came as a shock. No one had predicted the remarkable recovery she had made. Her physicians had recently given the girl a 95 percent chance of going home to her parents as a healthy child. Angela Lakeberg's brief life had not been a tortured existence of painful tests and tubes as some had originally imagined. Her heart had been adequately repaired by the surgical team and she never needed continuous painkillers. While in the hospital, nurses and volunteers had read books and played games with her. And Angela loved to smile and blow kisses.

But one day, Angela's temperature suddenly rose, and she began having trouble breathing. A blocked blood vessel was causing fluid to back up into her heart. Her doctors still felt she would recover when the little girl unexpectedly died.

Angela Lakeberg's death once again stirred the controversy over whether conjoined twins facing extremely serious medical obstacles should be separated at all. But Angela Lakeberg's doctors defended their actions, arguing that they took the best and most humane course of action. "We never believed it was a 1 percent chance. If we thought that it was not a reconstructable heart . . . we would have advised against it. We take long odds every day, but not crazy odds," a surgeon on the operating team said.[9] Mark Siegler, director of MacLean Center for Clinical Medical Ethics at the University of Chicago, echoed those sentiments when he said, "The baby's clinical course [recovery] supports the original judgment that this was a case they could deal with."[10]

Both sides present persuasive arguments on this issue. But while there are no clear-cut answers, one thing is certain. One way or the other, the outcome of the Lakeberg case will undoubtedly influence whether similarly conjoined twins are separated in the future.

CHAPTER 4

NOTEWORTHY EXAMPLES

In a number of cases, parents of conjoined twins have refused to have their children surgically separated. These parents may not be willing to risk losing either one or both of their babies during the procedure.

Some also fear that if separated, their children will have to undergo numerous painful and time-consuming surgeries to reconstruct vital organs.

At times, there may not be sufficient body mass between the twins for two separate people to comfortably exist. Therefore, such parents have instead taught their twins to lead the fullest lives possible while connected to each other. An example of this is conjoined twins Abigail and Brittany Hensel, whose daily lives are not unlike those of any young person their age.

Although the Hensel twins have two heads and two hearts, they share one two-legged body from the waist down. Their condition came as a surprise to their parents, Patty and Mike Hensel, who weren't even aware that they were having twins until they were born. But the couple adjusted quickly. Shortly after the girls' birth, the twins were rushed to a special children's hospital in a nearby city. "We thought they were going to die," recalled the girls' mother in describing the first few hours of the twins' lives.[1] But once they learned that their daughters were healthy and could adjust to a normal care routine, she noted, "We knew it would be fine."[2]

Abigail and Brittany Hensel share one two-legged body from the waist down. They have learned to work together for many tasks, such as tying their shoes.

45

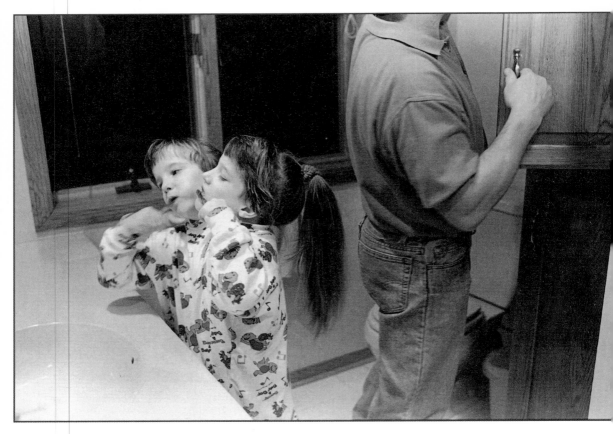

The Hensel twins brush their teeth as they prepare for bed.

Fortunately, the twins remained in good health as they grew. The only surgery required was to remove an awkwardly placed third arm between their heads. Because their circulation systems are linked, when one twin is ill, the other is affected. This means that Abby can take medication for Brittany's ear infection, and the

In many ways, the Hensel twins are no different from other children their age. Here, they are learning to ride a bike.

condition will clear up as though Brittany took it. The twins were especially delighted to learn that they only needed one set of vaccinations since that meant fewer shots to take between them.

While the two experience many things similarly, they are not completely alike. They may be hungry or feel sleepy at different times. Yet despite any contrary feelings they may have had through the years, the twins have learned to live harmoniously. They began walking at fifteen months of age without being shown who should move which foot first. Later on, they mastered swimming and bike riding.

Their parents decided against surgically separating the girls because their doctor had strongly advised against it. Mike and Patty Hensel knew that even if both girls survived the operation, they would face more surgeries, a great deal of pain, and lives in wheelchairs. Their mother put it this way: "If they were separated, they would pretty much cut them down the middle."[3] The girls' father added, "What kind of life could they have? They'd be in surgery for years, suffering all the time, and then they'd have half a body each."[4] Their feelings were reinforced by Dr. Benjamin S. Carson, director of pediatric neurosurgery at Johns Hopkins Children's Center in Baltimore, Maryland, who said, "It would make them invalids and there would be major emotional problems and psychological trauma. They've grown together. That's their way of life."[5]

The Hensels are certainly not the first conjoined twins to spend their lives attached. There are numerous instances of conjoined twins leading rich and enjoyable lives without being separated. These include

Abigail and Brittany with their class at school

Yvonne and Yvette McCarther, who before their death at age forty-three, had made many friends and accomplished a great deal. These young women had become outstanding gospel singers and toured the country with some of the top gospel groups. Always wanting to be independent, Yvonne and Yvette were proud of having been able to leave home and have their own apartment. At the time of their death, both were nursing-school students at Compton Community College in California. Paula Wilde, a spokesperson for the college, described the twins, "They were wonderful to be around. . . . They had an excellent sense of humor and spoke their minds freely."[6]

Presently, the elementary-school-aged Hensel twins do not wish to be separated. But their father notes that this possibility could be explored when they are older if they should change their minds. As of yet, however, adult conjoined twins have never been successfully separated.

Meanwhile, the Hensel girls are developing into unique and interesting individuals. Their school teacher has pointed out that each girl always does her own work. Despite the ready-made opportunity to copy one another's answers, they don't. Sometimes one twin will have the correct answer, but not the other. Their condition has further made them experts on teamwork and compromise. Once when an argument broke out in class, the twins led a discussion on the importance of getting along together.

At this point, it is difficult to say what the future holds for Abigail and Brittany Hensel. No one knows if the girls will marry as the famous conjoined twins

Despite being physically joined together, Abigail and Brittany Hensel are distinct individuals. Each completes her own homework and test papers.

Eng and Chang did. Presently Abby wants to be a dentist, while Brittany hopes to pilot planes. Since they can't be in two places at once, they will need to compromise. But so far, the Hensel twins have met life's challenges with remarkable success. And their mother feels that they are likely to do so in the future as well. As she said, "We don't need anyone to feel sorry for us. . . . If they [Abigail and Brittany] had to be put together, I think they were put together perfectly."[7]

GLOSSARY

CONCEPTION the act of becoming pregnant

CONJOINED TWINS twins born physically joined together in some way

CURIOSITY a person or thing that arouses interest

DICEPHALIC TWINS twins who have two heads but share one two-legged body

EPIDEMIC a widespread disease affecting many people

ETHICIST an individual who studies human conduct in an attempt to determine right and wrong

LIGAMENT a band of tough body tissue

MIDWIFE a woman who assists in the birth of a baby

SOURCE
NOTES

CHAPTER TWO

1. Janice Hopkins Tanne, "Free at Last," *New York*, November 15, 1993, 61.

2. CBS News 48 Hours, "Hoping For a Miracle," Transcript #360, January 25, 1996.

CHAPTER THREE

1. Anatasia Toufexis, "The Ultimate Choice," *Time*, August 30, 1993, 44.

2. Ibid.

3. Ibid.

4. Ibid.

5. Jean Seligmann, "Is It More Humane Not to Operate?" *Newsweek*, August 23, 1993, 44.

6. Ibid.

7. Elizabeth Gleick, "Problem Parent," *People Weekly*, September 6, 1993, 35.

8. Toufexis, "The Ultimate Choice," 44.

9. Anatasia Toufexis, "The Brief Life of Angela Lakeberg," *Time*, June 27, 1994, 62.

10. Ibid.

CHAPTER FOUR
1. Claudia Wallis, "The Most Intimate Bond," *Time*, March 25, 1996, 60.

2. Ibid.

3. Ibid.

4. Kenneth Miller, "Together Forever," *Life*, April, 1996, 55.

5. Ibid.

6. "Siamese Twins Buried in Specially-Made Casket," *Jet*, February 22, 1993, 16.

7. Miller, 56.

ORGANIZATIONS & PUBLICATIONS

BOOKS

Berry, Joy. **Every Kid's Guide to Being Special**. Chicago: Childrens Press, 1987.

Collins, David R. **Eng and Chang: The Original Siamese Twins**. New York: Macmillan Children's Group, 1994.

Miller, Marilyn F. **Behind the Scenes at the Hospital**. Austin, TX: Raintree Steck-Vaughn, 1996.

Rogers, Fred. **You Are Special: Words of Wisdom from America's Most Beloved Neighbor**. New York: Viking, 1994.

Rosenberg, Maxine B. **Being a Twin, Having a Twin**. New York: Lothrop, Lee & Shepard Books, 1985.

Shepard, Scott. **What Do You Think of You? A Teen's Guide to Finding Self-Esteem**. Minneapolis, MN: CompCare Publishers, 1990.

Suzanne, Jamie. **Three's a Crowd**. Lakeville, CT: Gray Castle Press, 1990.

Webster-Doyle, Terence. **Why Is Everybody Always Picking on Me? A Guide to Handling Bullies**. Middlebury, VT: Atrium Publications, 1991.

ORGANIZATIONS
Center for the Study of Multiple Birth
333 E. Superior St., Room 464
Chicago, IL 60611
(312) 266-9093

Twins Foundation
P.O. Box 6043
Providence, RI 02940-6043
(401) 729-1000

RESOURCES ON THE WORLD WIDE WEB

A detailed account of Eng and Chang can be found at this Web site. In addition to the description of their fascinating lives, this site also has lots of pictures. To find out more, visit:
http://www.infi.net/~leisure/brc/twins/twins.html

At **TWINSource**, you can find information about twins. Look under Twins in History for the section about Siamese twinning.
http://www.modcult.brown.edu/students/angell/ TWINSource.html

INDEX

Page numbers in *italics* indicate illustrations.

INDEX

INDEX

INDEX

ABOUT THE
AUTHOR

 ELAINE LANDAU has a Bachelor of Arts degree in English and Journalism from New York University and a Masters degree in Library and Information Science from Pratt Institute. She has worked as a newspaper reporter, children's book editor, and a youth services librarian, but especially enjoys writing for young people.

Ms. Landau has written more than one hundred nonfiction books on various topics. She lives in Miami, Florida, with her husband, Norman, and son, Michael.